FORENSIC INVESTIGATIONS
OF THE
ROMANS

Louise Spilsbury

CRABTREE
PUBLISHING COMPANY
WWW.CRABTREEBOOKS.COM

Author: Louise Spilsbury

Editors: Sarah Eason, John Andrews,
    Petrice Custance, and Janine Deschenes

Proofreader and indexer: Wendy Scavuzzo

Editorial director: Kathy Middleton

Design: Paul Myerscough, Paul Oakley,
    and Jane McKenna

Cover design: Paul Myerscough

Photo research: Rachel Blount

**Production coordinator and
    Prepress technician:** Tammy McGarr

Print coordinator: Katherine Berti

Consultant: John Malam

Produced for Crabtree Publishing Company by
Calcium Creative Ltd.

Library and Archives Canada Cataloguing in Publication

Spilsbury, Louise, author
        Forensic investigations of the Romans / Louise Spilsbury.

(Forensic footprints of ancient worlds)
Includes index.
Issued also in print and electronic formats.
ISBN 978-0-7787-4952-3 (hardcover).--
ISBN 978-0-7787-4958-5 (softcover).--
ISBN 978-1-4271-2118-9 (HTML)

        1. Rome--Antiquities--Juvenile literature. 2. Rome
(Italy)--Antiquities--Juvenile literature. 3. Forensic
archaeology--Rome--Juvenile literature. 4. Archaeology and
history--Rome--Juvenile literature. I. Title.

DG78.S65 2018   j937.00909   C2018-902989-7
                                        C2018-902990-0

Library of Congress Cataloging-in-Publication Data

Names: Spilsbury, Louise, author.
Title: Forensic investigations of the Romans / Louise Spilsbury.
Description: New York, New York : Crabtree Publishing, 2019. |
    Series: Forensic footprints of ancient worlds | Includes index.
Identifiers: LCCN 2018027898 (print) | LCCN 2018031061 (ebook)
    ISBN 9781427121189 (Electronic) |
    ISBN 9780778749523 (hardcover) |
    ISBN 9780778749585 (pbk.)
Subjects: LCSH: Forensic archaeology--Rome--Juvenile literature.
    | Forensic anthropology--Rome--Juvenile literature. |
    Excavations (Archaeology)--Rome--Juvenile literature. | Rome--
    Antiquities--Juvenile literature.
Classification: LCC CC79.F67 (ebook) |
    LCC CC79.F67 S65 2019 (print) | DDC 937--dc23
LC record available at https://lccn.loc.gov/2018027898

Crabtree Publishing Company

www.crabtreebooks.com   1-800-387-7650

Printed in the U.S.A./092018/CG20180719

**Published in Canada
Crabtree Publishing**
616 Welland Ave.
St. Catharines, Ontario
L2M 5V6

**Published in the United States
Crabtree Publishing**
PMB 59051
350 Fifth Avenue, 59th Floor
New York, New York 10118

**Published in the United Kingdom
Crabtree Publishing**
Maritime House
Basin Road North, Hove
BN41 1WR

**Published in Australia
Crabtree Publishing**
3 Charles Street
Coburg North
VIC, 3058

CONTENTS

Investigating the Romans   4

Solving Past Mysteries   6

Lost Roads   8

Pipe Dreams   10

Rock-solid Romans   12

Romans Come to Life!   14

X-ray Vision   16

Color Clues   18

Food and Fighting   20

Pills and Potions   22

On the Move   24

The End of an Empire   26

Forensic Future   28

Can Forensics Solve…?   29

Glossary   30

Learning More   31

Index and About the Author   32

INVESTIGATING THE ROMANS

Around 2,000 years ago, the city of Rome, in Italy, was the center of an **empire** that ruled more than one-quarter of all people on Earth! The Romans were one of the most powerful **civilizations** in history. But who were they and what do we know about them?

Solving Mysteries

Some of what we know about the Romans comes from written **evidence** they left behind, such as laws. We study Roman **remains**, such as buildings and bones. We also look at **artifacts**, or objects from the past, to find out more about Roman daily life. However, many artifacts are damaged, some are still hidden, and others are missing important pieces of information.

DID You Know?

The Romans were shorter than we are. By studying Roman skeletons, particularly the leg bones, scientists can figure out that the average Roman man was about 5 feet 6 inches (1.7 m) tall. The average American male is 5 feet 9 inches (1.75 m). But not all Romans were short. A third-century C.E. skeleton found near Rome in 1991 measured 6 feet 8 inches (2 m). That man would have been a "giant" in Roman days!

Archaeologists are using forensic techniques to learn more about the remains of ancient Roman buildings such as the Forum (above) in Rome.

Forensic scientists study skeletons to help detectives solve crimes such as murder. Forensic science can also be used to tell us about the bodies of ancient Romans, so that archaeologists can figure out how they lived and died long ago.

An example of missing important information can be seen in Roman paintings and skeletons. There are paintings of rich Romans eating, but none that show what food poor Romans ate. There are graves with ancient Roman skeletons, but most have no sign of any injuries. So, how can we figure out how they died? Is there a way to solve all these ancient mysteries? Yes—with **forensic science**!

HOW SCIENCE SOLVED THE PAST:

FORENSIC FOOTPRINTS

To solve crimes, forensic scientists examine evidence from the places where crimes took place, called **crime scenes**. The **techniques** that they use to solve crimes are also used by people to solve mysteries about the past. **Archaeologists** and **anthropologists** study the clues, or forensic footprints, ancient people left behind to find out more about them. Archaeologists use forensic techniques to find out about ancient buildings and **sites**. Anthropologists use forensic techniques to learn more about ancient people from their skeletons and the objects they left behind.

SOLVING PAST MYSTERIES

Forensic scientists can help police find a body in a recent crime scene and they can also find out where bodies were buried long ago. They dig up any items buried with the bodies, carefully make note of them, and **preserve** them. They then use forensic science to find out more about the bodies and items.

Raiding the Remains

Forensic scientists study skeletons or bodies to solve mysteries about a crime. They also study ancient remains to find out who people were and why they died. They can even use computers to create people's faces from ancient skulls.

So what clues, or forensic footprints, did the Romans leave behind and what can we learn from them? Let's follow the Romans' forensic footprint trail!

Scientists examine skulls such as this one, then use computer modeling to create an image of the person's face. The image can be incredibly lifelike and show us what the person may have looked like.

HOW SCIENCE SOLVED THE PAST:

MODELING MYSTERIES

We cannot visit the past, but we can model it. Archaeologists use clues from ancient sites to figure out how the buildings that once stood there looked. For example, **foundations** in the ground hint at walls. Pieces of broken pottery hint at garbage sites. Using this information, forensic scientists work on a computer to create a **three-dimensional (3-D)** model of the site as it might once have been. This helps us learn about how the buildings were made and what they might have been used for.

Forensic scientists can also use clues from the past to make 3-D models of people who lived long ago. They study skulls and skeletons to figure out what a person looked like. They then use that information to create a 3-D image of the person.

Archaeologists start by looking closely at artifacts, such as pieces of pottery from an ancient Roman site. They measure them carefully and try to figure out what they were used for. Then they carry out forensic tests on samples, or pieces, from the artifacts.

DID You Know?

Today, archaeologists are using cutting-edge forensic technology to bring Rome back to life! Using evidence from the ancient parts of Rome, they have rebuilt the city on computers and created a **virtual reality (VR)** world that people can enter. It shows how enormous the city was, and what its many buildings were used for. The Forum, for example, was a meeting and shopping place at the center of the city. There were also **temples**, where people worshiped their gods, and important buildings in which people ruled Rome.

LOST ROADS

We can still travel along routes of some ancient Roman roads, following in the footsteps of Roman armies on their way to take over new lands, **merchants** traveling to buy and sell goods, and messengers moving between cities. However, most Roman roads are worn away or covered over. Today, forensic scientists can use technology such as **satellites** to help us rediscover Roman highways that have been lost for many hundreds of years!

Looking with Light

Lidar devices fire **laser** light at a target, then measure the time it takes for the light beams to reflect, or bounce back. Forensic investigators use lidar to create amazingly realistic 3-D pictures of crime scenes, which they can study later in detail or use as evidence in court. Forensic scientists attach lidar devices to **drones** or aircraft. In flight, the devices send pulses of light into the land to create 3-D images of Roman roads hidden under forests or other obstacles. This can show us how long the lost roads were, how well they were made, and where they led.

Unlike this Roman road, many roads are still buried. Scientists use forensic technology to help them discover these hidden, secret roads.

Forensic science helped solve the mystery of where the Romans got the gold to make their coins.

HOW SCIENCE SOLVED THE PAST:

LASERS STRIKE GOLD!

The Romans loved gold. They used gold to make coins, jewelry, art, and other decorations. However, there is little gold under the ground in Italy. Also, most Roman gold found has a date after 200 B.C.E. So, where did all the gold come from? And why did it appear after 200 B.C.E.? Using lidar laser technology, scientists have discovered a huge Roman gold mine in Spain—the biggest in the whole Roman Empire. Rome had conquered much of Spain by around 200 B.C.E. Thanks to forensic technology, we now know that they were mining Spain for its gold.

As well as finding hidden Roman roads, we are also studying Roman artifacts to find out more about how these roads were made. This carving shows workers cutting down trees to clear a path for new roads.

Drones are small unmanned aircraft that carry cameras. They can capture images of areas that are difficult for humans to reach.

PIPE DREAMS

The Romans knew that people need a good supply of water to keep clean and healthy. To supply fresh water to **public baths** and places for washing clothes, the Romans cleverly built pipes and **aqueducts**, which are bridges to carry water over valleys. Drains carried away the dirty water and people's **feces**. Archaeologists have found pipes made of a **metal** called lead that date from around 10 B.C.E., but Roman cities had water supplies before then. What did they make their pipes from before 10 B.C.E.?

DID You Know?

The Romans may have used pottery as a kind of scratchy toilet paper! In 2012, a French anthropologist used forensic science to examine some pottery pieces from the site of a Roman palace at Fishbourne in England. He tested the pieces with chemicals and found some ancient feces on them. This meant the pottery could have been used as toilet paper—before this research, people thought the pieces were part of a game!

This mosaic shows a **slave** (right) handing his rich Roman master (left), a bottle of olive oil in a Roman bath. To clean themselves, Romans rubbed olive oil on their bodies, then scraped it off.

Secrets in the Soil

The answer was right beneath the archaeologists' feet! Each soil is **unique**, because each area of dirt contains a different mixture of ingredients. That is why forensic scientists can look at soil found on a shoe tread and link it to the soil at a crime scene. When soil scientists looked at soil from the Roman port of Ostia, dating back to around 200 B.C.E., they found tiny pieces of lead in it. This evidence proved that the Romans were using lead 200 years earlier than experts had first thought.

To **analyze** soil, forensic scientists may stain it with chemicals and look at it under a **microscope**. This can reveal parasites or parasite eggs that are so small they cannot be seen with the naked eye. Parasites such as these can cause serious stomach infections and were probably an everyday part of life for Romans.

HOW SCIENCE SOLVED THE PAST:

PARASITE PROBLEM

Despite their clean water supply, the Romans still had tummy troubles! A forensic soil scientist studying soils from ancient Roman toilets found evidence of **parasites** (small living things that live on or inside larger living things). Parasites can live inside the intestines of people, and show up in their feces. The soil showed scientists that Romans had parasites inside their bodies.

« parasite

ROCK-SOLID ROMANS

We can stand among the ruins of many temples, theaters, and other Roman buildings today. There are even complete buildings, such as a temple in Rome called the Pantheon. Like us, the Romans used a lot of a material called **concrete** (a mixture of gravel, sand, **cement**, and water) in their buildings. Amazingly, Roman concrete has lasted 2,000 years. That is longer than modern concrete will last. Why is Roman concrete so strong?

Zoom In!

Forensic scientists look through **electron** microscopes to see things in incredibly small detail. These powerful devices fire electrons at tiny things to make them look big. This helps forensic investigators spot tiny amounts of hair, clothing, gunpowder, and other substances that help solve crimes.

Electron microscopes can magnify (increase the size of) samples, including those from Roman buildings, by 100,000 times. This reveals details that other techniques cannot.

Uncovering the mystery of Roman concrete helps us understand how the Colosseum in Rome is still standing after 2,000 years.

When electron microscopes are used to zoom in on concrete from Rome, we can see its secret ingredients: **ash** from volcanoes, a white substance called **lime**, and lumps of volcanic rock. Today, builders use steel rods to **reinforce** concrete buildings. The Roman recipe for concrete was so tough that 2,000 years after it was built, the Pantheon's huge round roof, called a dome, is still the largest non-reinforced concrete dome in the world!

HOW SCIENCE SOLVED THE PAST:

UNBREAKABLE WALLS!

The concrete walls we build today on our coasts to hold back the sea do not last. They crack and have to be repaired or replaced within 100 years. Roman seawalls do not crumble! So, how have they lasted so long?

Scientists have used electron **probes**, or instruments, to analyze tiny samples of concrete from Roman harbors. Electron probes can be pushed into a solid object to show even the smallest amounts of chemicals it contains. The scientists discovered that when salty seawater mixes with the volcanic ash and lime used by Roman builders, it creates new substances that strengthen the concrete and make it waterproof. Today, builders are beginning to use this ancient Roman know-how to help them build stronger seawalls!

Forensic scientists studied the chemicals in the concrete of the Pantheon to find out what makes the material so hard-wearing.

DID You Know?

Forensic science can help tell us when Roman buildings were built. **Carbon dating** is a forensic technique used to find out the age of an object. Materials such as water and rocks contain substances called **carbons**. One particular carbon decays, or breaks down slowly, at a fixed rate, so scientists can measure how much of this carbon is left in an object to figure out its age. Scientists have tested samples of mortar (a mixture of sand, water, and lime used to fix stones together) from the remains of Vindonissa, a Roman army camp in Switzerland. The tests show the camp was built 2,000 years ago, around 15 C.E.

MAGRIPPALFCOSTERTIVMFECIT

ROMANS COME TO LIFE!

The ancient city of Pompeii, near Naples in Italy, tells us more about Roman life than probably anywhere else on Earth. That is because it was buried in a deep layer of ash when the nearby volcano of Mount Vesuvius **erupted** in 79 C.E. When archaeologists began to dig through the ash, 1,600 years later, they found a city frozen in time. Much of Pompeii has been very well preserved, including its wall paintings, jewels, coins, and even an oven filled with dozens of loaves of bread!

Bodies Lost in Time

Although many people escaped Pompeii when the Mount Vesuvius volcano erupted, around 2,000 people were killed. Over time, the ash around their bodies hardened, and the soft parts inside rotted away, leaving empty shells. Early archaeologists poured plaster into the ash shells to preserve the remains.

Teeth, unlike soft body parts, survive for thousands of years. They hold many clues for forensic scientists.

DID
You Know?

Romans in Pompeii had pretty good teeth! The bodies scanned at Pompeii show teeth in a surprisingly healthy condition. Scientists suggest this was probably because these Romans ate a diet high in fruits and vegetables.

When the volcano erupted in Pompeii, many people died together. Forensic study of groups of bodies helps us discover the connections between the people. Tests on the 13 bodies in this group revealed that six were from the same family.

This produced a 3-D plaster cast of the people, enabling us to "see" them at the moment of death. Unfortunately, the plaster made it impossible for modern archaeologists to see inside the bodies. So, they turned to forensic science. Forensic scientists can use **CT scans** of victims' bodies to figure out how they died. A CT scan creates detailed images of a person's insides.

Forensic finds

CT scans of Pompeii bodies have produced amazing 3-D images of the people. These include skulls and bones, and even hairstyles and clothes. We can now see much more clearly how old these Romans were, what they wore, and what they looked like. This helps us build a clearer picture of life in the city. The scans have even shown how the victims probably felt in their last moments, as the disaster happened. One young boy was found with his lips shut tight, holding his breath, trying not to breathe in ash.

HOW SCIENCE SOLVED THE PAST:

HOW DID THEY DIE?

Until recently, people thought that everyone in Pompeii choked to death when the city was buried in ash. However, CT scans revealed another shock. Many of those killed after the eruption died from serious head injuries, caused by falling rock or collapsing buildings. This forensic find proved that not everyone in Pompeii had choked to death after all.

X-RAY VISION

When the layers of ash were cleared from Pompeii's buildings, archaeologists were excited to discover many beautiful wall paintings, called **frescoes**. The frescoes had bright colors, which were perfectly preserved by the ash. However, the colors soon started to fade once they were exposed to the Sun, wind, and rain. Some frescoes almost disappeared. Were these valuable clues to Roman life gone forever or could forensic science help save them?

Finding the Frescoes

Forensic scientists use **X-rays** to find fingerprints and traces of drugs and explosives at crime scenes. The same technology is used to reveal secrets about the ancient past. X-rays are powerful, invisible waves of **energy**. In a fresco at Pompeii, thin beams of X-rays can show up tiny fragments of colored pigments, or substances used to make paints, that are invisible to the naked eye. The fragments can then be used to create a **digital** image of the fresco. This image can then be studied on a computer. Amazingly, using the technique on what looked like a dirty, blank wall revealed an image of a woman. It even helped experts figure out that a red pigment containing the metal lead was added to the woman to highlight her eyes. A black pigment containing the metal iron was used to sketch out her face and figure.

« This is a fresco from a house in Pompeii. Scientists use forensic techniques such as X-ray scanning to help them discover hidden parts of fascinating paintings such as this one.

HOW SCIENCE SOLVED THE PAST:

SECRETS OF THE SCROLLS

In an ancient library in the town of Herculaneum near Pompeii, piles of **scrolls** written by important Roman thinkers of the time were buried by the Vesuvius eruption. Many of these scrolls, some up to 50 feet (15 m) long, were so badly burned by the ash that they will crumble to pieces if opened. Now, archaeologists can peer into them using a special kind of X-ray. This has revealed text that was hidden for 2,000 years. At first, scientists could make out only the letters of the alphabet and a few words, such as "would fall" and "would say." However, they will eventually be able to read most of what was written on the scrolls. What more could the ancient writing tell us about the Romans?

Without forensic science, scrolls such as this one from Herculaneum would simply crumble and be lost forever.

Forensic science will help us preserve Roman remains such as this graffiti written on a wall. This will allow future generations to study them.

DID
You Know?

The Romans liked to write **graffiti** on walls! However, sunlight and weather are fast fading the graffiti. Before the writing is lost, scientists are using state-of-the-art cameras, similar to those used by forensic scientists to record evidence at crime scenes, to record what the Romans wrote. Some graffiti from Pompeii includes "Epaphra is not good at ball games," "Epaphra, you are bald!," and "Marcus loves Spendusa."

COLOR CLUES

In ancient Rome, just one glance at a person told you how rich or important they were. People showed off their high **status** by wearing colored clothing that was expensive to produce. Roman slaves had to grind up 14,000 insects to make just 3.5 ounces (99 g) of red **dye**! Poorer people wore plain-colored clothes because they could not afford bright clothing dyes. That is why the colors of people's clothing in paintings give archaeologists important clues to the past. However, the brightly colored paint that once covered many Roman statues has worn off. So, how can we figure out who was who in ancient Roman times?

HOW SCIENCE SOLVED THE PAST:

THE MYSTERY OF POMPEIAN RED

Many walls in Pompeii are covered in a famous color called Pompeian red. Scientists know that the color red was very expensive to produce because it came from a special kind of red lead. This metal was mined more than 1,500 miles (2,415 km) away. So, how could so many people in Pompeii afford something so expensive? Forensic scientists analyzed the chemicals in the red paint and found that some walls that now look red began life as a yellow color. The color was turned red by the **gases** that poured from Vesuvius as it erupted. Mystery solved!

Shining a Light on the Past

Forensic scientists have cameras that use **ultraviolet (UV)** and **infrared** light, or forms of light that we cannot see, to photograph crime scenes.

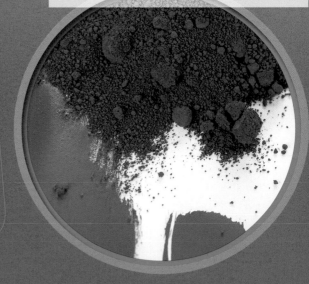

Forensic scientists can identify ancient Roman colors by testing tiny pieces of ancient paint.

Caligula was the Roman emperor from 37 to 41 C.E. On the left is a sculpture of Caligula's head. This is how the sculpture looks today. On the right is what the sculpture may have looked like in Roman times, before its paint wore away. Scientists used forensic techniques (see below) to find traces of paint that once covered the sculpture. They then used that information to color a copy of the sculpture.

Forensic cameras see things that we cannot see. Today, archaeologists are using UV and infrared light to analyze the surface of Roman statues. These forms of light reveal tiny traces of paint that was once impossible to see. This has helped archaeologists see the colors in people's clothing, and figure out how important they were.

DID You Know?

Purple was a powerful color in ancient Rome! Roman Emperors wore purple not just to look grand, but also because the color was expensive to make. Using forensic paint analysis, scientists have found that to make a tiny amount of purple dye, thousands of sea snails were boiled in giant lead pans for days on end. The poor workers who did this horrible job also had to suffer the terrible stink it created!

FOOD AND FIGHTING

There are paintings and writings that tell us how rich Romans ate wonderful feasts of meat, shellfish, cheese, fruit, and wine. But what did other Romans eat? How can we find out what ordinary Romans ate, or even super-fit **gladiators**, when there are no records of their meals? We turn to forensics! After a murder, forensic scientists analyze tiny fragments of different chemicals found in a victim's hair, teeth, or bones. This helps them figure out things such as what that person ate and where they lived. The same forensic science can reveal Roman secrets, too.

Take a close look at these gladiators. You can see that they are heavily muscled, but they are not very lean. Forensic scientists have analyzed the remains of gladiators to find out what they were eating to make them look like this.

It was important that gladiators had tough bodies—forensic analysis of their bones shows that these super-warriors were fed to fight!

WHAT'S ON THE GLADIATOR'S MENU?

Roman gladiators were men trained to fight to the death to entertain Roman crowds. Most pictures or carvings show gladiators as big, almost fat men, rather than slim, athletic figures. What were they eating to get so large?

It turns out that many gladiators were actually vegetarians! Evidence discovered by analyzing their bones and teeth shows that barley (a kind of grain) and vegetables, such as beans, were at the top of a Roman gladiator's menu. This was not because gladiators loved animals, however! Instead, to build up layers of fat, they ate a lot of **carbohydrates**—substances in food that provide heat and energy. This helped protect them from the blows of other gladiators. The food was washed down with a yucky "sports drink" of plant ashes and vinegar, which built up the gladiators' bones.

Secrets in the Skeletons

When ancient Romans sat down to dinner, little did they know that evidence of their meals would be captured in their teeth and bones thousands of years later! Today, archaeologists analyzing Roman skeletons can find chemicals from the food those people ate. Their analysis reveals that most poor ancient Romans ate simple foods such as bread and vegetable soup. They also ate a sloppy porridge made from a cereal grain called millet. Yum!

Forensic analysis of Roman teeth tells us that they ate mainly plain food. But they also ate more interesting foods, such as the figs shown in this ancient Roman fresco.

DID You Know?

You can tell what the Romans ate by looking at their feces! In Herculaneum, scientists have studied 750 bags of Roman poop taken from one sewer. They have discovered that some ordinary Romans had a much more varied diet than people previously thought. This included herbs and spices, such as dill, fennel, and pepper, and even spiky creatures from the bottom of the sea called sea urchins!

PILLS AND POTIONS

Some Roman writers talked about medicines and how to treat sickness. However, few Romans lived more than 50 years—and most died much younger than that. Very few ancient medicines survive, so historians have wondered if the Romans really did know very much about treating sick people.

Mystery Disks

In 1989, archaeologists working on a Roman shipwreck off the coast of Italy found some ancient medical equipment. Among the pieces was a tin box containing some flat, gray disks. No one knew what they were. In 2012, scientists took a slice from one of the disks and examined it, using **mass spectrometry**. This is a way of breaking down all the chemicals in something so each chemical can be individually examined. Forensic scientists can use mass spectrometry to find poison, or other clues, in the bodies of people who have been victims of crime. Archaeologists used the forensic technique to discover that the shipwreck disks contained the metal zinc. The Romans believed zinc could cure eye problems. Scientists now believe that the disks were probably ancient Roman pills, just like those we buy from a drug store today!

HOW SCIENCE SOLVED THE PAST:

ROMAN BEAUTY ROUTINE

Archaeologists working on a site in London, England, found a small pot that still contained some kind of creamy, very smelly substance. The cream had Roman fingerprints in it! It looked a little like face cream you can buy today. Could this be an ancient face treatment?

Scientists analyzed the cream and found it was made from animal fat, **starch** (see opposite), and tin oxide, which is a powder made from the metal tin. They then made a new cream from the same ingredients. They tried it on their own faces and found it was quite pleasant. It worked like a modern face cream. It showed that Roman women living in London during ancient times probably had beauty routines!

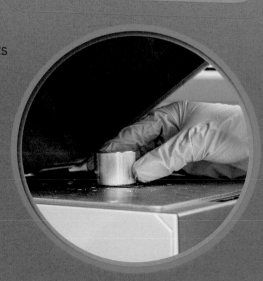

 Using mass spectrometry, forensic scientists discover what chemicals were in Roman medicines.

Forensic analysis of perfume in Roman pots can help identify the scent and the way it was prepared.

DID
You Know?

Roman women liked to look very pale! The forensic chemical analysis of the Roman face cream in London showed that one of its ingredients was starch—a substance found in plants and used to make a white powder. Starch makes things look white, and amazingly is still used in modern-day beauty products. The cream would have helped a Roman woman achieve a pale look—a sign she was rich and could stay indoors all day, rather than working outside like poor women!

We are learning more and more about Roman medicine from the study of their surgical tools, such as these, and the forensic study of the pills and potions that they used.

ON THE MOVE

Rome was the center of a huge empire, which was full of millions of people who called themselves Romans. Who were they? And where did they come from? Forensic scientists use a technique called **DNA** analysis on a crime victim's teeth and bones to find out where he or she was from. Could the same technique be used to track how far people moved within the Roman Empire?

Discoveries with DNA

DNA is a set of instructions found in every **cell** of the human body. It makes us who we are, including our eye color, hair color, and height. Analyzing DNA in bones and tooth **enamel**, which is the hard, white substance that covers a tooth, can help scientists figure out where a person was born. By comparing where a Roman grew up with where his or her body was found, archaeologists can figure out how far that person traveled.

The Roman army recruited men from all over the empire to fight battles and defend the empire.

DNA analysis of the skulls of Roman soldiers has shown that these men came from all over the Roman Empire.

Study of the chemicals in tooth enamel can tell historians a lot about a Roman skeleton. Chemicals in drinking water and food are captured by growing teeth during childhood. So, studying those chemicals and comparing them with chemicals in water and food in different places can tell us where a person came from.

HOW SCIENCE SOLVED THE PAST:

THE MYSTERY OF THE HEADLESS SKELETONS

A discovery of 80 male skeletons in a grave in York left historians confused. Who were they, where did they come from, and why did half of them have their heads chopped off? DNA has solved some of the mystery. Most of the men were from Europe, but at least one had grown up in the **Middle East**. They were all under the age of 45, with brown hair and brown eyes, except for one, who had blond hair and blue eyes. The men had grown up in poor households but were taller than average and had survived various injuries caused by weapons. Historians believe that these men may have been brought to York to fight as gladiators. Or they may have been criminals, beheaded for their crimes.

Some parts of the empire were as far as 1,000 miles (1,609 km) from Rome. DNA taken from skeletons has shown that soldiers traveled much farther from home than once thought. There were even Roman soldiers from Africa living in York, England.

DID You Know?

At the peak of the Roman Empire, about one million people lived in Rome. But they were not all born in Rome. Forensic analysis of the teeth from bodies in Roman burial grounds has shown how the diets of some people changed from childhood to later life. This means that many people who lived in Rome probably moved there as children, then ate what the Romans ate.

Close up, DNA looks like a twisted ladder. Forensic study of ancient DNA can unlock the secrets of Roman bodies.

THE END OF AN EMPIRE

The Roman Empire lasted hundreds of years, until it started to fall apart in around 476 C.E. There are probably a number of reasons why the empire collapsed. Some historians believe that a deadly disease called **malaria** was an important reason. Malaria is spread by an insect called a mosquito, and it still kills one million people a year. Roman writings mention a disease that matches what we know to be malaria. However, we do not know for sure that malaria contributed to the end of the Roman Empire. Can the forensic study of ancient Roman skeletons help us understand what happened to the Roman Empire?

DNA Detectives

Discovering the cause of death for any dead body needs careful detective work. Forensic scientists can take DNA from the bones and teeth of crime victims to figure out how they died. DNA studies of ancient Roman teeth have finally given historians the proof they need that malaria killed many Romans.

Thanks to forensic analysis of ancient samples, we now know that disease caused as many deaths as war did in the Roman Empire.

HOW SCIENCE SOLVED THE PAST:

WHO WERE THE BURIED BABIES?

In the 1990s, archaeologists dug up the skeletons of 47 children at Lugnano, north of Rome. All the children were less than three years old when they died. What caused their deaths? Forensic investigation has shown that the bodies were buried in around 450 C.E., toward the end of the Roman Empire. This turned out to be the largest Roman children's burial ground ever found.

Study of the soil in the graves shows that all the babies were buried within a few weeks of each other. Forensic scientists studying DNA taken from their bones discovered they all caught malaria during an **epidemic**. This is an outbreak of disease that sweeps through an area, killing many people very quickly.

Studying ancient skeletons helps us learn about ordinary Romans who do not appear in written records.

Malaria spread easily because of the movement of Romans throughout the empire. It was also spread when foreign armies attacked Rome. So malaria was probably partly responsible for the fall of the Roman Empire.

DID You Know?

The DNA taken from the children's skeletons at Lugnano is the oldest evidence of malaria in history. The name "malaria" comes from the Italian *mal aria* or "bad air." It was also known as "Roman fever."

Forensic science has proved that the mosquito was as deadly in Roman times as it is today.

FORENSIC FUTURE

We may never know all of the details of how the Romans lived, but forensic science techniques are helping us learn more than we ever dreamed possible. While artifacts and remains give us clues to the empire's past, forensic tests provide archaeologists and anthropologists with hard evidence. Advances in technology are finding clues that we never knew existed, and providing a fascinating gateway to the past.

What might forensic technology uncover in the future? With every tiny piece of the puzzle that is discovered and fitted into place, this fascinating science is making our picture of life in ancient Rome clearer!

DID
You Know?

Hidden deep beneath ancient Rome is a secret network of tunnels. These tunnels carried water to thousands of fountains, baths, and pools in the city. Experts are now using 3-D laser scans to map the structures and investigate how they were made. So far, they have found that Romans built curved sections in their water systems to slow down the water's flow. They have also discovered that the Romans used teams of diggers, who started in opposite directions from each other. They dug until the two teams met in the middle. Rome's engineers really were incredible!

What else might we learn in the future about Roman gladiators with the help of forensic science?

CAN FORENSICS SOLVE...?

Here are two of the great still-unsolved mysteries about ancient Rome and the Romans. Forensic scientists are using forensic footprints to try to solve these mysteries, too!

Lost Soldiers

For years, people in the remote village of Liqian in northwest China were mystified by the fact some villagers had Western features, such as green eyes and blond hair. Rome did not spread its empire into China, but an old local story suggests that the villagers are descended from a lost Roman **legion** that did settle in the area. Could this be true? DNA testing of the villagers has shown that almost two-thirds of them had ancient ancestors who were white-skinned and European. Further DNA analysis of villagers and artifacts may solve this mystery at last!

Doubting the Dates

Mount Vesuvius, the volcano that destroyed Pompeii and Herculaneum, erupted on August 24, 79 C.E.—or did it? Some experts now think it might have happened later in the year. Chemical analysis of pots from stores and warehouses show that they contained freshly harvested fall fruits, such as pomegranates and walnuts. CT scans of the body casts of victims in Pompeii also show that they were wearing layers of warmer clothing. Did the eruption take place in the fall rather than the summer? Using forensic techniques, experts hope to solve the mystery once and for all.

Could future DNA studies prove that Roman soldiers traveled as far as China?

GLOSSARY

Please note: Some **bold-faced** words are defined where they appear in the book.

analyze Study something carefully

anthropologists Experts who study who ancient people were, how they lived, and where they came from

archaeologists Experts who study where ancient people lived and the things they left behind

ash Dust or powder left after a fire

carbons Chemicals found in all living plants and animals

cell The basic building block of all living things

cement A powder mixed with water and other ingredients to make concrete

channels Long, narrow spaces that are dug into the earth and through which water flows

civilizations Settled and stable communities in which people live together peacefully and use systems such as writing to communicate

digital Where information, such as a picture, can be seen on a computer

DNA Material that contains all of the information needed to create an individual living thing

drones Unmanned aircraft guided by remote control or onboard computers

dye A substance used to change the color of something

electron An extremely small particle of energy

empire A large area of land or group of countries ruled over by one leader

energy Power that can be taken from something and used

engineers People who design and build complicated things, such as bridges and harbors

erupted Exploded with huge power

evidence Facts and information that tell us if something is true

feces Poop

forensic science The use of scientific methods and techniques to find clues about crimes or the past

foundations Solid structures that support a building from underneath

frescoes Paintings in which the paint is applied to wet plaster

gases Substances, such as air, that have no shape and are usually invisible

gladiators Men trained to fight other men or wild animals in an arena

graffiti Words drawn or written on a wall

laser A narrow, concentrated beam of light

legion A unit of 3,000–6,000 Roman soldiers

lime A white substance used in making concrete

merchants People who buy and sell goods in large amounts, especially by trading

metal A substance, such as gold or lead, which is found underground and can be melted and turned into useful or valuable objects

microscope A device used to see objects that are too small to be seen by the naked eye

Middle East The countries of northern Africa and southwestern Asia, from Libya to Iran

preserve Make sure something stays the same

public baths Bathing areas that anyone can use

reinforce Make stronger

remains Bodies, bones, objects, or parts of objects left over from the past

reservoirs Artificial lakes for collecting and storing fresh water

satellites Machines in orbit around Earth that collect information or are used for communication

scrolls Long, rolled up pieces of a kind of thick paper called papyrus

sites Places where something is or was

slave A person who is owned by another person and has to work for and obey that person

status A person's position, importance, or rank in relation to others

techniques Methods of doing particular tasks

temples Buildings where people go to worship their god or gods

three-dimensional (3-D) Having or appearing to have length, width, and depth

unique The only one of its kind

virtual reality (VR) A 3-D, computer-generated world that can be explored by a person

X-rays Waves of energy that are usually used to create pictures of the inside of the body

LEARNING MORE

Books

Croy, Anita. *How Did Rome Rise and Fall?* (Mysteries in History: Solving the Mysteries of the Past). Cavendish Square Publishing, 2017.

Malam, John. *Ancient Rome Inside Out* (Inside Out). Crabtree Publishing Company, 2017.

Randolph, Joanne, (ed.). *Living and Working in Ancient Rome* (Back In Time). Enslow Publishers, Inc., 2018.

Stokes, Jonathan W. *The Thrifty Guide to Ancient Rome: A Handbook for Time Travelers.* Viking Books for Young Readers, 2018.

Stoltman, Joan. *Looking for Clues with a Detective* (Get to Work!). Gareth Stevens, 2018.

Websites

www.ducksters.com/history/ancient_rome.php
The Ducksters education site has lots of information about ancient Rome, including daily life, family life, homes, and cities.

www.natgeokids.com/uk/discover/history/romans/10-facts-about-the-ancient-romans/#!/register
Learn ten amazing facts about ancient Rome at the National Geographic Kids site.

www.pbs.org/empires/romans
Based on the television series *The Roman Empire in the First Century*, this site explores every area of life in the Roman Empire, including family life, home life, gladiators, social status, and the part played by Roman women.

www.sciencedaily.com/news/fossils_ruins/archaeology
Visit the ScienceDaily site to discover the latest forensic science discoveries in archaeology. The site also has a section on anthropology.

INDEX

anthropologists 5, 10, 28
aqueducts 10
archaeologists 4, 5, 7, 10, 11, 14, 15, 16, 17, 18, 19, 21, 22, 24, 27, 28
armies (foreign) 27
army (Roman) 8, 13, 24
artifacts 4, 7, 9, 28, 29
artwork 9, 10, 16, 17, 19, 20, 21, 23, 28
ash, volcanic 13, 14–15, 16, 17

beauty products 22, 23
beheadings 25
birth place 24, 25
bones 4, 5, 6, 7, 14, 15, 20, 21, 24, 25, 26, 27
buildings 4, 5, 12–13
burial grounds 25, 27

Caligula 19
carbon dating 13
cause of death 5, 6, 15, 22, 26–27
channels 8
children's burial grounds 27
clothing 12, 15, 18, 19, 29
coins 9, 14
colors 16, 18–19
Colosseum 12
concrete 12–13
crime scenes 5, 6, 8, 11, 12, 16, 17, 18, 22, 24, 26
CT scans 15, 29

diseases 25, 26–27
DNA testing 15, 24, 25, 26, 27, 29
drones 8, 9
dyes for clothing 18, 19

electron probes 13
enamel (from teeth) 24, 25
engineers 8, 28

fall of the empire 26–27
feces (poop) 10, 11, 21
foods and diet 5, 14, 20, 21, 25, 29
forensic footprints 5, 6, 29
Forum, the 4, 7
foundations 7
frescoes 16, 21

gladiators 20–21, 25, 28
gods 7
gold 8, 9
graffiti 17

height 4, 25
Herculaneum 17, 21

lead (metal) 10, 11, 16, 18, 19
legion 29
lidar 8, 9
Liqian 29

malaria epidemic 26–27
mass spectrometry 22
medicines 22, 23
merchants 8
microscopes 11, 12, 13
models of buildings 7
models of people 6, 7
mortar 13
mosaics 10
mosquitoes 26–27

olive oil 10

paints 18, 19
Pantheon 12, 13
parasites 11
perfumes 23
pigments 16
pipes 10

plaster body casts 14–15
Pompeii 14–15, 16–17, 18–19
Pompeiian red 18
pottery 7, 10
public baths 10

reservoirs 8
roads 8–9

scrolls 17
sculptures 19, 20
sea walls 13
skeletons 4, 5, 6, 7, 21, 25, 26, 27
skulls 6, 7, 15, 24
slaves 10, 18
soil analysis 11
soldiers 24, 25, 29
Spain 9
starch 23
surgical tools 23

teeth 14, 20, 21, 24, 25, 26
temples 7, 12
three-dimensional (3-D) models 6, 7
toilet paper 10
toilets 11
tunnels 28

Vesuvius, Mount 14–15, 16–17, 18, 29
virtual reality (VR) 7
volcanic eruption 14–15, 16–17, 18, 29

water systems 8, 10, 28

X-rays 16, 17

zinc 22

About the Author

Louise Spilsbury loves researching new information on a wide variety of subjects. She has written more than 200 books, some co-authored with her husband Richard, on a range of topics from art and ants to zippers and zoos!